MONUMENT ETERNAL

MONUMENT ETERNAL

BY
ALICE COLTRANE
(A. COLTRANE-TURIYASANGITANANDA)

AKASHIC
BOOKS
BROOKLYN, NEW YORK

Published by Akashic Books
©1977, 2025 Alice Coltrane (A. Coltrane-Turiyasangitananda)

ISBN: 978-1-63614-225-8
Library of Congress Control Number: 2024940652
Second Akashic Books printing

Originally published in 1977 by the Vedantic Book Press,
Los Angeles, CA

EU Authorized Representative details:
Easy Access System Europe
Mustamäe tee 50, 10621 Tallinn, Estonia
gpsr.request@easproject.com

Akashic Books
Instagram, X, Facebook: AkashicBooks
info@akashicbooks.com
www.akashicbooks.com

*This book is selflessly presented
to my truly sacred
Supreme Lord*

Table of Contents

Foreword to the New Edition   *9*

Foreword (Original Edition)   19

Preface   *23*

Introduction   *25*

Chapter 1 SPIRITUAL RE-AWAKENING   *27*

Chapter 2 AUSTERITY   *33*

Chapter 3 SPIRITUAL PERCEPTION   *45*

Chapter 4 REALIZATION   *55*

Chapter 5 THE LORD'S GRACE   *63*

Foreword to the New Edition
by Ashley Kahn

onument Eternal is the first of five books written by Alice Coltrane-Turiyasangitananda. She completed it in 1977 as a way to chronicle and make sense of the intense personal transformations she experienced between the years 1968 and 1970. She reports that it was an "assignment," even calling it a "divine command." That's how the book opens, and then one realizes she's writing of experiences she underwent at the same time the world around her had rocketed into the fast lane, a time when the velocity of social and political change had hit top gear—a time when our heads were left spinning, and everybody had stories to tell. Yet her story was a singular one even by the standards of the late 1960s—in the jazz and music scenes, in the world as a whole. It still stands out—and it offers a way of understanding a life that still shapes and influences today, a life of devotion and service.

During this period, to those on the outside looking in, Alice Coltrane was already a hero of sorts, a prodigious female pianist who had broken through most of the barriers women faced in what was primarily a man's world. She had risen to renown—from the end of 1965 through 1967—as a member of the group led by her famous husband, John Coltrane. After his passing in July '67, she continued to ascend. Within a year, she had learned to play harp and, enabled by a recording studio in her basement that she had overseen the construction of, launched a record label and released music she had recorded with her husband. Then she kicked off her own career as a leader with a series of well-received recordings on the well-known Impulse label, all recorded in her home studio, establishing a sound all her own: a kaleidoscopic, one-world blend of modal and spiritual jazz, church music, the blues, Indian ragas, and Hindu songs of praise. By 1970, the world regarded Alice Coltrane as a woman who had not only transcended tragic circumstances, but had thrived after being left a widow at the age of thirty with four children and a weighty name that placed her permanently in the spotlight with the burden of expectation.

Little did we know. As Alice Coltrane relates in *Monument Eternal*, her reality during this period was filled with lonely nights of self-doubt and tempestuous fears, with voices and visions. She writes about pain and weight loss and a doctor visit and the suggestion of self-harm. There are descriptions of her family being alarmed and coming to visit, a sister staying with her, and her young children sleeping when she could not. She writes honestly and openly about her inner turmoil less than seven years after it happened, yet finds it necessary to explain the long delay: "I had let [it] go without a concrete manifestation for many years." (Intriguingly, John Coltrane had offered a similar apology in his liner notes when he completed *A Love Supreme* seven years after he intended to.)

In *Monument Eternal*, Alice Coltrane makes sense of the suffering as a process of purification and self-testing. She calls it "mental and physical austerities," and uses the Sanskrit term *tapas*. Her words reveal a rapid inner shift, loosening an exclusive relationship with the Black church and a growing dedication to a Vedic spiritual path—Advaita Vedanta, to be specific—that would lead her to her chosen mission in life, eventually forgoing an active music career in order to establish an ashram. What began with readings and discussions with her husband and friends in the early 1960s led her to study on her own, and in 1968 she met and came under the guidance of Swami Satchidananda, an acolyte of the pioneering and prolific guru Swami Sivananda. Satchidananda was among the first wave of Indian gurus to arrive in the US in the 1960s. His gospel was one of yoga and Vedanta, and he was asked to deliver the opening benediction at the legendary Woodstock festival in 1969. In late 1970, Alice Coltrane followed Satchidananda for the first of a number of trips to India, furthering her initiation as she dug ever deeper into a monastic life.

Interestingly, despite Satchidananda's exceedingly important role in Alice Coltrane's life journey (her fourth album is titled in his honor), he is only mentioned and does not figure prominently in *Monument Eternal.* In her book, Alice Coltrane's personal path—from darkness to light, from sacrifice to physical and spiritual well-being—is what matters most. That, and an abiding sense of discovery, bliss, and individual purpose: the idea of surrendering to a divine will, of being part of the plan. In one of the book's most joyful, poetic moments, she relates a number of times when nature and the world of man intersect and make sense in relation to each other. She explains, "The Lord said, 'The morning birds that sing so sweetly are "out of a job" when there are no children to wake up.'"

* * *

Monument Eternal also brings to mind another John Coltrane parallel that deserves to be emphasized. As a universalist who—like Alice—grew up in the Black church, the saxophonist espoused more of a philosophy than a specific path on the 1964 spiritual self-declaration *A Love Supreme.* "All paths lead to God," he wrote in the poem that graces the LP cover; he played the album's four-note motif in all keys to musically represent that idea. While one doesn't find the word "Jesus" on *A Love Supreme*, he did not turn his back on his Christian upbringing, but rather incorporated its purest teachings—and other belief systems—into his own amalgamated vision. By 1966, John Coltrane was still in spiritual process, defining his universalist truth and how best to describe it, and avoided using even the word "God" in an interview with students on his only trip to Japan:

> *Question: I believe you are a Christian, but what kind of God, is it, in your mind?*
> *Coltrane: I don't know. I don't like to try and define God. I think he's beyond any definition that I can give.*
> *Question: And you think you know there is a god.*
> *Coltrane: I feel something.*

Alice Coltrane accompanied her husband on that trip. In their brief four years together, she and her husband spoke at length and shared all aspects of their spiritual awakening and self-education. And Alice embraced her husband's principles of universalism and inclusion. That Alice embraced a preexisting system of worship in which to house this philosophy was her own choice, and one she knew might require explanation. In an interview for *Essence* magazine in 1971, she stated, "The Western Church has failed, especially with young people. It was set up to serve needs it's not meeting. Ask a Swami Hindu monk or someone else from the East about life after death and you'll get answers that are real about direct experience, about looking to God. It has helped me to go on."

By 1988, Alice Coltrane's dissatisfaction with her initial religious path was somewhat less pronounced, with the essential message of Christianity woven into a more universal Vedic point of view. In a radio interview that year she said:

> *The Eastern philosophy gives the aspirant the chance or opportunity to develop himself . . . Somehow the experience that I had, and I'm not going to speak for everybody, I'm speaking for myself . . .*

you go there and you hear the service and you get the instructions: prayer, to be faithful, trust, ask God's blessings. Yet it never tells you what you can become—more Christlike, more Christ-conscious! [But] the church says get under that. Be less than [Christ].

I'm not stating we should be more than Christ, but you know, really. He says you have a higher, a greater potentiality. "I've fed five thousand. I want you to feed five million!" To get self-realization. To get self-actualization, fulfillment. That's the point. And it isn't selfish—that term. It just means that you go to your fullest and highest potential, and not be limited by some tenets of some doctrine that says that we come here, here's the minister, and that we pay our tithes and go home and go back to your job or business or whatever and do everything you want.

Monument Eternal captures the beginning of that self-actualization—the promise of what Alice Coltrane was to become. Not long after the tumultuous years she describes in the book, she adopted the Sanskrit name Turiya Aparna and relocated her family to Southern California. Later, to match her decision to become a swamini in her own right, she lengthened her name to Turiyasangitananda, meaning "the Lord's highest song of bliss." By 1979, Alice Coltrane was all in: she stopped touring and recorded the live album *Transfiguration* in Los Angeles that would be her last commercial release for almost twenty-five years. In 1983, she bought property in an idyllic, isolated section of Agoura Hills, where she built the Sai Anantam Ashram, leading a spiritual community until she passed away in 2007. Part of the ashram's administration was focused on releasing music she recorded for her followers and on publishing her writing—including *Monument Eternal.*

I was honored to meet and speak with Mrs. Coltrane a number of times. (I referred to her as "Mrs. Coltrane" the first time I met her in 2001; her "Swamini" honorific I learned to use later.) Our initial meeting is the memory that is etched the deepest. It took place in the modest office of Jowcol Music, the music publishing company her husband first established in the late 1950s. It was located in the business district of Woodland Hills, California, in a small strip mall adjacent to—if memory serves—a nail salon and a Thai restaurant. An unlikely location for what was to be a conversation about John Coltrane, *A Love Supreme*, and other matters of cosmic and enduring importance. I had prepared how best to arrive. I decided on a new white shirt and trousers, not jeans, and brought flowers—not cut blossoms but a potted plant. A living offering made more sense.

She was dressed in a bright-orange, wraparound Punjabi dress and received me warmly. She sat behind a small desk with myself in a chair across from her. Again, I recall the dissonance between our focus and the location. Other than a palpable feeling of benevolence that enveloped the room, it could have been a job interview for a start-up. I placed my recorder on the desk between us and we began.

Ashley Kahn is a music historian and author of A Love Supreme: The Story of John Coltrane's Signature Album.

Foreword (Original Edition)
by Shankari Carol Adams, M.Ed

Alice Coltrane-Turiyasangitananda is widely known as an accomplished musician. She has concertized on piano and harp in Carnegie Hall, Lincoln Center, and other leading music halls throughout the world. More recently her energies have extended into writing. And as a spiritual teacher, she is engaged in instructing her students on meditation and spirituality. Turiyasangitananda has written an abridged documentary on her spiritual life in this book entitled *Monument Eternal* which tells of her spiritual initiation, revelations, and austerities.

Although my recent reading of the book inspired me, the greatest impact was my first reading of the manuscript several years ago. My spirit was elated. At the time, I was seriously searching for a greater spiritual understanding of life. Various approaches to spirituality, such as institutionalized religious associations, and the science of extrasensory perception failed to quench my thirst for knowledge. The joy derived from reading this book is simple to explain: the author was concerned about spiritual life. Her concern was not intellectual. It was of the heart. She states that "Several years ago . . . I felt the deepest transcendental longing to realize the Supreme Lord."

The book encouraged my quest for spiritual freedom, for it shows that everyone is potentially capable of realizing God. Individually, people differ according to family background, abilities, culture, but underneath such surface diversity is a sacred relationship every soul has with God.

Monument Eternal is other than a sublime discourse because it is not entirely devoid of implications for practical application. The book invites us to examine our own lives. It reminds us that we are more than the physical body; we are eternal spirit-souls, and as such, we should feel encouraged to cultivate faith and render loving service to the Lord.

In short, Turiyasangitananda's book, *Monument Eter-*

nal, is a story of her unwavering devotion to God, and her receiving of the immemorial blessings of His Grace. May this moving account of a soul's spiritual experiences inspire each of us to awaken the divinity within us.

Shankari Carol Adams, M.Ed, is the author of Portrait of Devotion: The Spiritual Life of Alice Coltrane, Swamini Turiyasangitananda.

Preface

There has come to my being the most auspicious time to fulfill a divine command, one which I had let go without a concrete manifestation for many years. This command is an assignment and an honor for me to write: a book based upon the soul's realizations in Absolute Consciousness and its spiritual relationships with the Supreme One. I am deeply and truly thankful, and I will be eternally grateful to the great Sovereign Supreme Lord, always and forevermore.

Turiyasangitananda
(Alice Coltrane)

April 4, 1977
Los Angeles, California

INTRODUCTION

During the year of 1970, the Supreme asked that I prepare the manuscript for this book. Most of the revelations occurred between the years of 1968 and 1970, although recent disclosures have been presented herein.

I intended to release it last year, however by Supreme request I was to prepare it for publication this year.

The book is divided into five chapters: The first chapter views some of the spiritual and theoretical aspects of elements, nature, human and other living creatures and how they individually relate to the Supreme Reality.

Chapters Two and Three chronologically tell of my spiritual initiation, revelations, austerities, and spiritual experiences.

Chapters Four and Five culminate into more spiritual

revelations: a look into several past lifetimes, my bringing certain persons before the Supreme Presence, the mentioning of some of the names of the Supreme Lord as my principal Initiator throughout my existence, and the receiving of the Lord's Grace: I, then, humbly endeavor to give an accounting of some of my most transcendental, blissful associations with the Supreme.

Monument Eternal is a book about my true spiritual experiences, and spiritual suffering which has never ceased even unto this present day.

CHAPTER ONE

Spiritual Re-awakening

he Supreme Lord inspired the creation of the physical, mental, and etheric bodies in man, and the construction of the lower animal, vegetable, and mineral kingdoms. Each intelligence received the blessing of an atomic, cosmic, primal element of life and love.

Research into the primordial substance of matter and spirit reveal the atom to be like a small universe, with the same characteristics as a major solar system. Not unlike the sun, each atom independently contains within itself a great play on magnetism and harmony. The feminine electrons hold a powerful sway over the masculine protons inside the atom. There also exists within each particle of atomic energy a supreme and irrefutable universal order of Absolute Consciousness. This clarifies to my being the reason that even the smallest atoms in existence can never be destroyed—when bombarded, or cut by force, they only transform themselves. For example, the atoms in a decaying piece of wood could someday become petrified rock or coal, among other things.

The sacred triple expansion of the Supreme Lord, which has its infinite properties of creating, maintaining, and dissolving, pervades the entire atomic and atmanic[1] universe. In reality, the proton, electron, and neutron are none other than the Father, Son, and the Holy Ghost in minute form—the Holy Trinity hidden beyond the veil of human awareness. This holy triune universal support is also known as the Supreme Lord in three persons: Brahma, Vishnu, Siva; and in mundane terminology it is called Power, Light, Energy.

In view of the unspiritual and undivine direction in the lives of so many people on this earth, the Lord often tells the spiritually awakened ones about divine light and universal love, by stating to them that "Mother Earth loves to feel your bare feet upon her breast; the wind loves

---

[1] *atmanic*: pertaining to the soul

your face, your hair . . . the sun loves the measurements of your back; flowers and other plant spirits rejoice upon receiving natural rain, or water. Trees swing and sway with joy when I assume the form of the initiating spirit who will bring forth the blossoms of spring and the fruits of summer." It was my great privilege to stand in a tree and witness just such an event. The long limbs of a huge fruit tree swung back and forth rhythmically, in response to the Lord's Supreme touch.

When speaking of humanity, the Lord said, "I know you and love you. You are my divine light."

When speaking of other living creatures, the Lord said, "The morning birds that sing so sweetly are 'out of a job' when there are no children to wake up."

One dawning—around six a.m.—I could hear a single bird singing and flying all alone.

I asked the Lord, "What is the bird saying?"

"It is saying 'wake up' to all the other birds."

An immediate polyphonic incantation filled the air. I asked, "What is their response?"

"It is 'thank you.'"

Several years ago, following a long period of elementary meditating and reading of some of the diverse books on spirituality and world religions, I felt the deepest transcendental longing to realize the Supreme Lord. This longing within the depths of my heart was soon acknowledged, for within a short period of time I experienced the first rays of Illumination and spiritual re-awakening. On the physical plane these radiations opened new avenues of awareness in the brain cells; even subtler were the inner effects of light and the cognizance of a spiritual revelation taking place within me.

This wonderful revelation was brought about by the power, compassion, and mercy of the Supreme Lord— who has myriad attributes, such as an infinite variety of names, forms, formless manifestations, and innumerable expansions. The Lord's limitless modes of expression, disclosures, and direct communications always manifest in my being as pure consciousness, knowledge, and divine wisdom. Often upon inception of the Supreme light, the force of the Lord's energy acting upon the human psyche as such, delivers the spiritual Illumination simultaneously with the profound ordeal of *tapas*, or austerity.

The procedures of *tapas*, which encompass every aspect of spiritual and physical suffering, have to be endured. And they are sometimes endured beyond human comprehension, to the extent that one's mental and physical state appears to be devoid of and shut off from Supreme protection—which is not true—and diminishing in health and strength due to the frequency of the *tapas* that has to be performed.

A human who is going through the austerity aspects of a spiritual revelation must be able to withstand the effects of purification, which is analogous to the processes and the results of empirical chemistry performed by an alchemist who transmutes base metal into gold. By fire, the Supreme Alchemist transmutes base metal—i.e., the human heart—into gold. The Divine Assayer tests gold by scrutiny . . . When all the dross is burnt away, and by analysis the gold's purity has been confirmed, an individual's heart will have become purified in love—bright and shining in a splendor of divinity like the purest gold.

Aside from the workings of alchemy, I had to endure many operations of penance, austerity, renunciation, sacrifice, and suffering. Trials and conflicts were created to test strength and endurance, measure and weigh all spiritual faculties, capacity, and tenacity of the soul.

The mental and physical territories had to undergo a purificatory spiritualization to bring about the expansion and heightening of my consciousness-awareness level.

Such purification, although highly beneficial to the soul, is not entirely for the sake of the individual, and does not really benefit the Supreme Lord. True devotees of the Lord do not have to be tested or taught anything, because such devotees are always willing to be tested and prepared for any position of service renderable unto the Supreme for the sake and benefit of others.

CHAPTER TWO

Austerity

or more than 600 million years of human life, the Supreme Lord has gently instructed me in the ways of *tapas. Tapas* means miseries, or austerities. *Tapas* means mortification. It is also the taking upon one's self of a voluntary suffering for some spiritual good. *Tapas*, when it is a benediction of mercy, will elevate one to the highest level of transcendental, loving service unto the Lord. The Supreme Lord initiated me, beginning with the word *tapa* or *tapas*, unto His highest disciplic Order, the transcendental Order of *Shakti*[2] Initiates. *Tapas* was then and still is the gentlest call from the Supreme One to my being to render loving, devotional service unto Him.

---

[2] *Shakti* is Energy. It does not refer to Lord Siva, nor to Tantra initiates in this context.

Last year I received from the Supreme a very special and highly sacred communication. The communication was of a confidential nature. Recently, it has been sanctioned that I may disclose it herewith as it correlates the aforementioned:

The Lord who is the Supreme controller of everything, who controls the memory and forgetfulness of all living beings, recalled my memory to a time many eons ago before the dawn of this creation when He caused an impenetrable darkness to cover the whole of space. The darkness also sufficiently concealed His wonderfully brilliant effulgent light which was radiating the brightest illuminations in all directions.

The Lord then directed my attention to a place where I saw the helpless figure of a humanlike being stalking around in the dark. He appeared to be the pitiable result of severe *tapas*. He looked bewildered and pathetic. His body was so devastated he could not stand up. The Lord said to me:

"Do you know him?"

"No, I do not . . . When will his *tapas* be finished? Who is he?"

"It is over. He has just completed 1,000 celestial[3] years

---

[3] One celestial second is equal to one solar year or one 365-day calendar year.

of *tapasya*. He is My instrument. He will be the Creator of this universe."

The figure in the gloom of that dark night seemed to be lonely and apprehensive of something unknown. Eventually, he spoke, saying, "When I can stand up"—he was halfway up, previously he had been down as I have also been down during *tapas*—"I shall begin meditating."

The Supreme Lord initiated the Creator beginning with the appropriate prerequisite *tapa* or *tapas* before he could receive his education in the science and art of creating, and after the successful termination of his suffering austerities, he was ready to be taught by the Supreme Lord exactly how to create this universe. The Creator is also an Initiate of the Vedic *parampara*, or disciplic succession.

My *tapas* in this lifetime initially began with increased waking hours and extended meditations. Long fasts were maintained and sleepless vigils endured. Extensive mental and physical austerities caused my body weight to fall from 128 to 105 pounds within a few weeks; later it was reduced to 95 pounds.

The physical *tapas* consisted of a series of examinations on my reactions and aversions, specifically to heat and cold, light and darkness, life and death, joy and sorrow—i.e., on the dualities of life—polarization. Some of the materials used in the tests included metals, glass, wood, chemicals, oils, plant fibers, and waste materials. There were examinations by water—hot and cold; by air—as in levitation; by heat—as fire; and by earth—as dirt.

My heart was stopped several times a day, and sometimes the heartbeats shifted to the right side of the body. All the hair on my head sometimes stood on end as if it were being electrically charged. *Mauna*, or silent intervals, and the length of breath retention were timed.

There were periods of isolation and separation from my family and friends, as well as humiliating and self-effacing austere sacrifices performed before the presence of relatives and persons known and unknown to me. All the comforts of home were prohibited, and the discarding of personal belongings and possessions went without exception.

During an excruciating test to withstand heat, my right hand succumbed to a third-degree burn. After watching the flesh fall away and the nails turn black from the intense heat, it was all I could do to wrap the remaining flesh in a linen cloth to keep it in place. Later that day, the right arm atrophied for a short period of time, but it was soon restored to normal.

During another similar examination, the left hand became partially burned.

Whenever metals were introduced into a test, more often than not they entered my body. Marked from head to toe, the greater part of my body resembled the stigmata of a crucified person—blood issued from almost every part of it.

The physical tests continued for several weeks, finally yielding to the mental ones, which hovered around like gray clouds in the atmosphere. The mental tests impress directly upon the mind, or astral body, and upon the etheric and causal bodies within man. They are of a graver, more profound nature than the physical ones, and the results of such investigations determine the advancement, development, and prowess of the soul.

The mental tests began with radiations directed upon the mind: Such things as electronic elementals, cosmic sounds, astral explosions, intrafractory rays, oceanic and abyssal waves, astral earthquakes, subterranean shocks, and etheric sirens were brought to bear upon it. There were meetings and confrontations with both disembodied souls and phantasmagoric entities with astral deformations.

I was astrally projected from the physical body very

frequently, practically every day, and permitted to travel from plane to plane. Occasionally, I was projected from the second-stage, "twin" astral body, the carbon copy of the physical, into a subtler third-stage etheric body, which is a bluish-white or silvery ectoplasmic apparition of the astral body. There were projections into a fourth-stage causal body, which is transparent and circular in form. It resembles a clear, round globe, and is absolutely devoid of all human parts and extremities whatsoever—no arms, legs, or face are present. There is one more projection, one which might be considered as "being in the image and likeness of the Lord" without form. It is Absolute, Manifested Formlessness. It is the highest and the most supremely subtle one. It positively defies discovery and description. It is irrefutably Unrefutable. It transcends all the material atoms and material energy. It is a pure consciousness in which one experiences the Real, Eternal, Supreme Consciousness—the complete and unconditional Absolute Sovereignty of the Lord.

Lessons on astral navigation were included among the tests. There was forward and reverse flight, also vertical and horizontal. My astral body was always in an upright position; this made standing descents at enormous rates of speed feel devastating. It was like the downrush of a falling elevator.

In an astral body, you can fly through glass, through the brick wall of a building, or through any material obstruction, without pain or impact. And you can move on air, smoothly and swiftly, without stepping and foot-pedaling like a human being.

There were transmigratory experiences, which were somewhat like rehearsing for one's own funeral. The Lord usually made these performances of death and resurrection quite pleasant and etherically beautiful. This transition called death is a soft, tranquil graduation . . . When viewing my body lying in state, I never feel sorrow or sadness. Instead, I actually feel the deepest humility and appreciation for the genius and excellence of the Supreme Lord.

I encountered some astral beings. They exhibited a very marked increase in their vibrational rate. When they spoke, their lips did not move; yet they were verbally communicating to me from their face or brain area, and at a faster rate than the ordinary human.

When I was confronted by a malefic, demoniacal entity, or just a plain mischievous spirit, its appearance seemed to be more caricaturistic than surprising.

Ironically, the behavior of the astral bodies of some

living persons was noticeably worse than that of the deceased ones. And, to my surprise, they at times would attempt to smother, or inflict some harm to my astral body. Such efforts on their part availed them nothing, for I found the astral body to be quite invulnerable to attack or injury.

Notwithstanding the above, my physical body succumbed to the sound of planetary ether. Its spinning sound whirled and revolved so strongly inside my ear that I fell into an unconscious state. When the waking consciousness returned, I would stand up . . . The whirling sound would then return again and bring my body down to unconsciousness. This occurred three times in succession. During the last occurrence, I fell to the floor into shattered glass which had earlier been used in a test. Some of the glass got wedged into my skin, although at that time I had not realized that I was mentally transcended above pain because I did not discover the glass in my skin until three days later when I removed it.

A state of fearlessness followed this course of events, accompanied by an increasing concern for the welfare and safety of others, although self-concern and personal matters were of little or no importance to me. It became very difficult to react to anything, whether the case were happy or sad. This difficulty or aversion to reaction also produced my inability to shed even a single teardrop. The Lord had to automate such a thing by creating a sensitivity around my eyes, from which streams of tears flowed plentifully; yet there was not a trace of an emotional disposition in me.

A supreme spiritual law does not permit for the defeat or endangering of any of the higher sheaths within man during *tapas*. This immutable law, unfortunately, does not apply to the physical body. Consequently, bodily injury is at times inescapable.

The cleansing and purifying processes used in this revelation were found to be a real, true intonation, which lifts the mind up to its highest possible levels of harmony, awareness, and receptivity. The Holy Spirit does not enjoy residing in an unclean heart. Yet this Divine Spirit is in all beings; otherwise they could not exist. However, the vehicle, or the house of the Divine Spirit, should be kept pure and clean.

My relatives became extremely worried about my mental and physical health. Therefore they arranged for my return to their home for "care and rest." On the contrary, the intended care for me never took place due to my total abstraction and detachment from the family. As for rest—during a three-month interval, I never slept for more than two hours a week.

Also, my relatives sincerely and unsuccessfully tried to bring me back to my former consciousness. Actually, communicating with people was found to be like a suffering judgment. In fact, it was almost impossible for me to dwell upon earthly matters, and equally impossible for me to bring the mind down to mundane thoughts and general conversations.

Next there came a period of learning, unlearning, and spiritual re-learning. During this study, I had to memorize a tract or one whole revolution of some unfamiliar subject matter. Upon learning it, I had to mentally repeat it several times around at rates of speed up to approximately three hundred words per minute.[4] After this was accomplished, I had to reverse the whole process, going counterclockwise, and mentally repeat it backwards at the same rate of speed.

The result of this practice promotes one to a high level of mental preparedness. For example, you become readily

---

[4] This kind of repetition can more than quadruple when it is practiced astrally.

adaptable to all types of change, or conditions, ready to chart a new or alternate course; alerted to encoding and decoding techniques; ready to abandon traditions, prepared to sever any attachments, prepared to discard or renounce everything.

The night revealed many of its secrets to me. For instance: the ectoplasm of the spirit bodies of my sister and her son—during their sleep—floated several feet away from their physical bodies. Their spirits vibrated like flags in the wind. One evening, I was sitting down on the children's bed; their dog was asleep in the room. I became projected from my physical body, and as my spirit arose, I called the dog's name out loud. When the dog saw my spirit, he cowered and fled, frightened, into the nearby hallway. Upon my re-entry into the physical form, I immediately went into the hallway to see if the dog was still alarmed. Fortunately, he was found to be all right. Sometimes, the earth's rotation could be felt, and walls could be seen moving forward and backward.

One night, something roared and groaned continuously. It sounded as if it were a nether entity whose subcontrabass bellow descended beneath the range of human hearing; this made it inaudible to the ordinary human ear—except for one instance. I am certain that my sister heard this unusual sound, because it suddenly rumbled and roared, very strongly. She covered her ears and said, "I think . . . I am hearing things!" and made a gesture for everyone to become silent. She then composed herself to hear better. Such silence was of no avail, for apparently the sound had escaped her hearing completely. This groaning went on without relief for several days, twenty-four hours a day. It seemed to be coming from the base of the floor, or from some subterranean place. One other night, a higher-pitched version of this same sound impacted so forcibly against the windows, I suspected that there might be broken glass, although upon checking the windowpanes, they were found to be intact.

CHAPTER THREE

Spiritual Perception

When looking through the spiritual eye, or the third eye encased within the human mind, one can see vividly beyond the ken of human eyesight, beyond the material atom, and into the future, thereby transcending the limitations of time and space. Here are a few explanations: While observing the development of a child, it could be seen changing from an infant to a teenager, within seconds, and sometimes reverting back to an infant, within seconds. A middle-aged man was seen changing into an old man, and finally into a corpse. A rug that had once been a polar bear's skin got up and walked away as an animal again. I observed a modest head of hair grow into thick, long tresses of hair, instantly. Flowers were seen growing and blooming instantly, like pictures of plants taken with a time-lapse camera. Some of the flowers grew as tall as trees. Some of the blooms were multicolored.

When focusing on a photograph of anyone or anything, by will alone the picture can be made to animate, to come to life. It will change expressions, smile, wink. While focusing on the photograph of a holy man[5] who had an elephant, and who was fond of animals, I wanted to see him in a setting where he would be caring for horses. Right before my physical eyes, the photograph changed into a pastoral scene. The saint was bringing food and water to the horses. He carried a large water vessel. After watching him serve the older animals, I wanted to see him serve the little ones, the babies. By looking a little to the left of the saint, I observed the most precious little weanling colt following him.

A household animal entered and ran through the house. Its body was transparent—one could see right through it. It entered the room I was in, exited, and was never seen again.

Images were reflected off doors, floors, draperies, walls, and other surfaces; even a television set, if not in use, could become a proper receiver and transmitter of images from the Supreme.

---

[5] Sathya Sai Baba

One evening, my sister went into her room and closed the door. As I approached, not thinking anyone was inside, I turned the knob and walked in—to her utter astonishment. Upon entering the room she had locked the door from the inside.

One night, the house was perfectly still and quiet. All the lights were out. The Lord said, "Turiya, you shall taste sugary-fire." After a considerable length of time passed, the moment finally arrived. Very suddenly, a lightning bolt coming from the ceiling struck against my physical body. The silvery flash of light lit up the room, yet it was so subtle that it barely could be felt.

On another night, gold and silvery fire flamed brightly atop a bookshelf in my room. After a while, it finally burned itself out; yet there was not a trace of smoke, charring, or damage to be found. Later, I observed another fire blazing inside my being. It started in the chest area . . . I was up to my neck in flames. Much later, the Lord said, "Look at your feet." I looked down—everything was sanguine; my feet and toenails had all turned blood-red.

Throughout the course of events, my physical frame grew increasingly thin and emaciated; my facial features changed slightly, and to some people my face was beyond recognition. They questioned my relatives to ascertain of my identity. My brother, a man in his middle thirties, cried pathetically upon his first sight of me. Also, a dear youngster who used to assist in the household cried sorrowfully when an ambulance came for me.

The worst injury sustained was to my right hand; and immediate medical attention became necessary. The physician who treated the hand actually recoiled at the first sight of it, as might a novice.

While under the doctor's care—for about ten days— my mind continuously transcended pain and suffering altogether. The taking of doctors' prescriptions or other medications was prohibited. If a doctor would administer a pill to me, I would never ingest it. Eventually, I would be left alone, and I would, at such time, properly dispose of it. The Lord would not permit the entrance of chemical medications into my body. The wonderful healing life-breath of the Lord would freely enter and strengthen it. It fortified my entire being. It would flow in the form of ringlets into either my mouth or ear—softly billowing downward into my abdomen, then down into my feet. When it reached the farthermost point, it would bounce slightly, and slowly begin its ascent upward toward the brain. Operating topically, this same life-breath would daily exercise the injured hand—taking and massaging each finger carefully, one at a time.

There were instances in which the sleeping consciousness and dream sequences of the children were revealed: When the children were asleep without a dream, they all emitted a long sustained buzzing sound similar to that of a bee. When they dreamt, their visions could be seen in the clearest detail. For example, once the oldest son, then three years old, was asleep on his bed. In his dream, he was playing in a field of flowers on a beautiful summer's day. The sky was blue and clear. He was jumping around happily and playfully. When the youngest son was only two months old, during his sleep I saw and heard him mentally repeating the word "I" continuously, as if chanting an affirmation or a mantra.

Not only could the thoughts of people be heard, they could also be seen. Sound and thought vibrations could be seen coming from a distance, traveling through the streets, on up through the window, and into my room. This recalled to my mind a time when the beloved John Coltrane Ohnedaruth, shortly before his final departure from the earthly plane, told me of *Akasha*. *Akasha* is the universal memory file cabinet of the universe. The thoughts, words, and deeds of all people spontaneously pour into this file, continuously. Ohnedaruth said that the file is usually positioned a few feet away from a person. However, if there are two or more persons present, the file would then be situated in the center of the room or area. The file also photographs and records each vibration, movement, and articulation of an individual.

Nearing the end of the earth-tenure of Ohnedaruth, who was a great musician and composer, he was often given to leaving his physical body. He was at times away from it for hours. Occasionally, he would speak of his interspheric travels.

Swami Sivananda, the great Indian saint of the Himalayas, established a large ashram and hospital in the foothills of Rishikesh, India. Although he was discarnate at the time, Sivananda appeared to me almost daily; and he was often seen with an entourage of celestial beings.

During a special ceremony, I assumed the form of a young child. In this way, Sivananda could hold me upon his arm, as you would hold an infant. He also held a plate of *prasadam*, or sacred food. He then fed small portions of the food to me from his hand. Finally, he said, "After you finish your reading, 'come upstairs.'" He meant come up to higher revelations.

One day, while in a spiritual form, I stood with Sivananda outside his ashram in Rishikesh. I then heard the Lord say to me: "Someday you shall have a Vedanta school." Today, that "school" is a reality. The Lord laid the foundation stone for it several years ago. It is now called the Vedantic Center.

During Sivananda's lifetime, he initiated many of his disciples into the renounced order of life, known as *sannyas*. One such soul is Yogiraj, Swami Satchidananda. During my travels with him through India and Sri Lanka (Ceylon), I found him to be a gentle leader and selfless servant of humanity.

In the afterlife, Sivananda is a director-in-chief of one of the nether worlds. A major duty of his is to direct disembodied souls into purgatory. His powerful chant alone draws the newly departed ones unto this just expiatory state. This place is known as "El Daoud."

During the preceding days, there transpired a period in which the laws of retribution and recompense came to the fore. It began with a review of my former misconceptions of past lives followed by a thorough re-examination of the errors made by humanity during the days of antiquity. Despite the fact that the Supreme wanted man to be made in the image of God, with the face and voice of God, a crest-jewel in the crown of creation—man's forgetfulness of his spiritual self and his dangerous attachment to sense gratification are the principal factors that produced the moral decay on this earth, the loss of spiritual sovereignty and values, and the decline into decadence and ignorance.

It has been reported that when death approaches, your whole life flashes before your sight. It is true, except that my review showed only the difficulties of human life—and consequently, at no time during these reviews were there scenes showing any spiritual achievement whatsoever. Only the negativisms of human life were shown.

Next, a period of vocal recollections ensued. A vague statement made from my person, many years ago, was replayed incessantly. It was not known at the time of the deliverance of the utterance that at some future date, the identical words would be resurrected from the dead and continuously resounded inside my ears—like an infinite broken record—for hundreds upon hundreds of days.

The great prophet Mohammed, in one of his earlier dispensations, spoke of a period in his lifetime which parallels this experience. He stated that "from a single word spoken idly, I had to hear for an eternity."

The processes and treatments used in *tapas* command respect. Their effects are often mistaken for wrath and punishment, which unfortunately is a poor understanding of spiritual purification. Such mistaken ideas should not occupy the thoughts of anyone's mind, nor should any acts of mortification or self-effacing penitential programs be entertained. For even though the destination is one, the roads that lead to spiritual realization are many.

One of the greatest mysteries hidden behind the scenes of human intelligence is the existence of an unconditional state of Perfection. In truth, it is a state which surpasses genius, or the highest forms of intelligence imaginable. It is a state of perfect peace, which is unchecked and unlimited by time and place—with their judgments of death and decay. It is a state in which a truly liberated soul knows that it is a part of the great cosmic body of the universe—an eternal being, a spiritual sun of the magellacosmos,[6] transcendental, spatial—soul of the Supreme Soul.

In this state, my eyes see only the true Reality which supports this universe, and also the things which remain concealed beyond the ken of the human mind. This per-

---

[6] The Magellanic Cloud galactic systems are located near our heavenly galaxy and contain our earth and solar system, and they are situated about three hundred thousand million light-years away from the next spiritual-material universe.

fection and freedom can be experienced not only in the heaven worlds, outside or around this universe, but right here on earth.

CHAPTER FOUR

REALIZATION

On the remaining pages, I shall try to relate to you, to the best of my ability, exactly what Cosmic Consciousness, Nirvana, Illumination, Absolute Consciousness, or Self Realization is. And I will try to give some insight as to what a soul's universal transcendental and personal relationships can be like with the Supreme Lord (even though each soul will experience the Lord in a similar, yet different, secret, ever-new way).

This Absolute Consciousness and realization of the Supreme affords a kind of freedom in which the soul lives and moves around like a sovereign of this universe. When engaged in devotional service unto the Supreme Lord, an individual is like a perfect being of this earth, as well as of the heavens. It is also that indescribable state of manifested formlessness in which one can function within and beyond the smallest atom. Principally, when manifesting as such, a soul can bodilessly, defying detection, follow and move alongside people without their knowledge or discovery; and can easily attune to their mind or heart—sense their pain, suffering, or joy, and experience the expressions of their art or profession. A soul can function in at least four places at once in this wise.

When you travel around the earth in your spirit-body, without the use of machines, you actually stand on air, and travel faster than the speed of thought. The earth . . . its form, its dimensions . . . looks so peaceful from above . . . When traveling through some of the astral worlds, I find a beauty that is rarely seen on this earth. The health and vitality of departed souls from this earth is remarkably good. Men who had died in their old age, such as my father, who passed away in his middle sixties, and the genius of avant-garde classical music, Igor Stravinsky, who also died in his old age, had the vim and vitality of men in their early thirties—handsome, energetic, powerfully built. They looked almost exactly as they had looked as elderly men, except for the fact that neither man's face showed old age, wrinkles, folds, or age lines.

When I see my mother—she passed away in her old age—I observe a woman whose beautiful face beams with youthful loveliness and health. Her skin tones are rich and glowing, its texture soft. If ever she communicates to me on a subject of great importance, her face is not stern or grave. And the reason is that there are no indentions or frown lines built into the forehead. Therefore a pleasant countenance always prevails.

On another plane of existence, boys and girls appeared to be undifferentiated; that is, the girls could sit as free as a boy or a child might, without any feelings of indignation or embarrassment.

The hair on the heads of some of the people looked as if it were sprinkled with diamonds. It sparkled like stars in the night.

Many planets which shine like stars in the heavens appeared condensed from their usual size. Once, during the night, I watched a tiny beautiful star aglow on my windowsill approximately three hours before dawn. The Lord said, "Bid it come to you." Mentally, I asked the little star to come to me. It would not move. I made a few more attempts. Again, it remained adamant. Actually, it could make no approach to me because of my slower vibratory rate during the waking consciousness. When the dawn broke, I physically lost sight of it. A deep meditation followed, at which time the Lord attuned my vibratory radiations to an adaptable level. Then there came a pleasant surprise! In the clearest detail, I observed this very same tiny star occupying a seat on my lap.

On another evening, a star of larger and greater dimensions appeared. Its illuminations were very bright, yet soft, to the physical eye. Its whole periphery radiated a warm golden-yellow light. It was about twenty feet away from me.

The raising of the sacred *kundalini*, the fire energy at the base of the spinal column, to the thousand-petaled lotus in the brain, is also a part of this very same Consciousness—Realization. Physically, when this fire is released, usually its force and heat are too fierce to be endured in the waking state. The Lord had to put me to sleep before its ascent. Although physically asleep, my back was on fire, and aching with pain. Suddenly, my spirit leaped out of me and stood ceiling-high, away from the burning body.

The mysterious *kundalini* deposits upon the ascetically initiated millions of keys which unlock the doors to many of the mysteries of life. *Kundalini* energy also transcends the lower nature, and it brings the soul into consummation with the Supreme Lord.

One may gain insight into the functions of the lower kingdoms of horses, birds, and other animals as well. You can visibly see into their character and background, as well as view scenes showing any defects, deficiencies, or special abilities.

Some birds built a nest beneath the roof of our patio. Curious little boys would on occasion climb a ladder and look inside the birds' nest. Upon their approach, the mother bird would always fly away. One day, I noticed that the nest, the mother bird, and her eggs were all missing. By concentrating, I found out that the bird had left with her unborn for another location due to her fear that a human hand would destroy them.

If ever our dog needs worming, small fish-like creatures can be seen floating around inside its stomach.

It is also possible to experience the mental processes of animals and insects by meditating upon them for the purpose of observation, investigation, or research. From the mind alone, one can experience the thought movements and brain mechanisms of the lower intelligences.

On the subject of reincarnation, scenes from several different incarnations were shown of some of my previous lives. In the lifetime before this one, I saw pictured the life of a simple, home-type personality in the feminine form . . . Nearing the end of her life, she died during a successful effort to save the life of a child. In another existence, my spirit was again in the body of a woman. She was a frail quiet person. Death, which overtook her in her middle age, was due to a pneumonic condition. One of the earlier incarnations illustrated a short life of a boy in ancient Egypt. The birth took place in the family of Ptolemy and Cleopatra in Alexandria. They named the child Ptolemy III. Ptolemy was the son of Ptolemy II, the king of Egypt. Earlier ancestors of the Ptolemys included kings and queens, mathematicians, geographers, and astronomers. Ptolemy was an excellent young musician who played a large golden harp inside the marble courts of the palace.

Today, in our home, we have many musical instruments. They include two grand pianos, woodwinds, drums, two organs, a guitar, a vibraphone, a violin, flutes, a koto, a sitar, a tamboura, and four harps.

Ptolemy loved the sound of the harp—oceanic, deep billowing . . . Ptolemy could never internally absorb or digest food properly; consequently he died in his youth at the age of twelve.[7] In the postmortem condition, he

---

[7] He died from a disease known today as cystic fibrosis, which is still threatening the lives of little children of this day and age.

looked quite majestic and regal with his head set back like a little king.

At another time I was born 532 years ago in India. At the age of thirty-five I became a *sannyasin* and was studying Vedic literature along with some of my brother disciples. Lord Chaitanya,[8] who was living on the earth at that time, was under twenty years of age and had not yet taken *sannyas.* He selflessly, after a long period of deliberation, entered into the renounced order of life for the purpose of demonstrating the perfect example of an ideal *sannyasin*, and to establish his identification with the Supreme Lord. I knew that Lord Chaitanya was the personification of endless knowledge and the enjoyment embodiment of the Supreme One in three persons, and that final liberation was certain for me. Yet I often pondered many, many days and nights over returning to this relative plane, and witnessing it on the level of the ordinary human being again, as I had done in the past. By my own vote, I elected to come back to this earth. I know of only two *sannyasins* who have stated that they liked returning to the earth. However, at this point in my existence, I no longer entertain any personal thoughts whatsoever with respect to

---

[8] Lord Chaitanya, also known as Krishna Chaitanya Mahaprabhu, was a great saint and spiritual teacher. He was born in 1486 in Sri Mayapur, Bengal.

earthlife, or spiritual life beyond the level of transcendental service unto the Lord.

One of the highest experiences of my existence occurred about 500,050 years ago, during the Dvapara Yuga, the period of time which was before this Kali Yuga. I received transcendental Vedic knowledge direct from the mouth of Bhagavan Lord Sri Krishna.

CHAPTER FIVE

THE LORD'S GRACE

The possibility of levitation presented itself. For example, one day my physical body was carefully lifted up and delicately transported from one room to another. Another time, preparations for levitation began with an involuntary self-inflating action, purposed to lift and move the gross body. When the demonstration was over, the body slowly began to deflate.

I found spirit-levitation, or invisible transfer, to be the best method of transportation, due to the physical body's inability to pass through material objects, and its inadaptability to high atmospheric pressure. Astral beings travel as fast as the speed of thought. The Supreme Lord can move us faster than the speed of thought. And here is the principle: There is an infinite storehouse of mind-substance, where atoms of thought-materials exist in a fragmentary form. Before the conception of a thought, these particles of mind-substance simply collect and are without any positive form or identification. When you are inspired with a thought, the particles of mind-cells formulate, and conception—the basis for all thoughts—begins. Next comes the awareness of the conception, which is a feeling within the heart. Soon the mind perceives; then it mentally sees. So, if an astral being thinks of traveling to a city in the East, or elsewhere, the astral body can reach the destination as fast as it takes to think the thought. Moreover, souls moving in an absolute form, made in the image and likeness of the Supreme Lord, are already there. The Lord asks us a question in an earlier Revelation, saying, "If I am in all places, at all times, where can I move?"[9]

Being with the Lord is better than being with friends or a loved one; and it is so much better than married life. And the reason is simply that the Lord is always around you twenty-four hours a day, a constant companion who is continuously awake and alert; never sleeping—not even for a single moment—consistently powerful, and always

---

[9] This question refers to the omnipresence of the Supreme who is the sole support of all universal manifestations, yet He is limitlessly everfree, aloof, and transcendental to it all.

at the zenith of empyreanic supreme strength. And, because of this closeness, I do not know what loneliness is, nor do I know what it feels like to be lonely, for I am never alone.

One day the Lord said, "Ask of me a boon." I thought over the question for a while. Realizing that I could think of nothing that I really wanted, I said, "Thank you, but I don't want anything." The Lord said: "I shall give you a boon. It shall be freedom from karma, freedom from your actions." What this means is: a person who is free from karma is like one who makes a mark on the air or on the water. Such a soul is not bound to or by any action, and is even free from the results of any action, be it honor or dishonor, increase, decrease, joy, sorrow, merit, demerit. It also means that such a soul is fully liberated from activities. So, no matter how much work a free soul engages in, he or she is never bound to or by its results.

The Lord is the only true physician, true friend, true parent(s), true teacher. The Lord's face(s) is the only real beauty to behold. Also, the Lord can change faces and forms like people change clothes.

The Supreme One—the best and only great musician—can render multitudes of choirs of angelic singing and symphonies of sound literally from out of the air. The choral voices have a range that is higher and deeper than the human voice; and they are not constrained to breathing before, between, or after phrases. Moreover, the Lord can produce sound from such non-musical entities as motors, electrical appliances, clocks, dishwashers, refrigerators, cars, airplane engines, windowpanes, water, trees, the wind, and from people—without their knowledge. I once listened to a great musical play on melody and rhythm during the sleep of some relatives. Their respiratory rate increased while they slept, and their out- and in-going breath became a vehicle for sound and song. Six people sounded as if they were one hundred strong. Effects of cymbals, bells, tinkling percussion, and dialectic inflections—if the songs were of a foreign origin— were clearly audible.

Many of the celestial musical instruments can be played without the use of hands or any physical contact whatsoever. Your mind, your heart, is your only approach to them. Your thoughts open up the many avenues of sound and expression on these wonderful instruments.

Practically every night, I was permitted to play a "psaltery." Unlike the ancient one, it had full orchestral range, and could be played at phenomenal rates of speed and volume—without awakening anyone—while the floor and walls vibrated from the force of it.

During that time, I had never seen the psaltery.[10] The Lord said: "Only four souls in this creation have seen it. You will be the fifth one." . . . When hearing the names, I found them all to be outstanding ones. They included two musicians and composers (Handel and Bach), Sri Aurobindo[11] (an all-informing source of the universe), and the fourth name was found to be the most outstanding one of all; it is the name of the great prophet and Savior, Jesus Christ.

The Lord has brought me into the presence of angels, *devas*, cosmic gods and spiritual Beings, such as Totu Puri, Fatima, the Virgin Mother Mary, Aurobindo, Sivananda, Ramakrishna, Gotama Buddha, and Jesus Christ.

Stations were established in my body then, and they are active centers today. They only receive positive and negative signals. They do not transmit or transfer signals. These centers are most active when I am contacting the

---

[10] *Psaltery*: as of recent days, I have seen this instrument.

[11] *Sri Aurobindo* or *Aurobindo*: here refers to an information transmissions spiritual agent and not to the spiritual matter of the Pondicherry ashram in India.

outside world. They are located in the feet, lower legs, hands, eyelids, and in the ears.

Seeing the Lord emphatized is another wonderful aspect of the Consciousness-Realization. The Lord will appear and communicate to you through such a diverse variety of forms as rocks, flowers, electricity, water, rain, air, wind, and trees—trees in this condition actually sing. They have a tone, a quality, and a hum that is unlike any kind of man-made instruments heard on earth.

The Lord will also appear in various human roles—most of which are readily recognizable to me—such as a uniformed guard, a police officer, a sentinel, a lifeguard, a musician, an aviator, a physician, an elderly person, or an infant, and will easily appear to you in a very special way that is not unlike your very own family or self—knowing your mannerisms, your expressions, and speaking the language or dialect peculiar to your heritage or culture.

Before entering into the conclusion of this book, I would like to take this opportunity to mention the names of my Supreme SatGuru who has initiated me in this lifetime and in many other lifetimes. 7,000 years ago and 3,000 years prior to that time, it was Lord Vishnu (Krishna).

In this lifetime it was the Supreme as well, although He appeared to me throughout my life in partial expansions of other spiritual personages and in elemental expansions of fire, or light, up until nine years ago when He initiated me unto his sacred judgment and holy name. He was in the form of Bhagavan Sri Ramachandra.

Sri Rama was the Supreme Revelator, prime motivator, and Supreme director of all that has been divinely revealed herewith in the form of this book. Although today, I am presently serving the Supreme in His original spiritual form.

The Supreme One is a great giver of such presents and gifts as sweets, fruits, flowers, and ambrosia; an eternal wellspring, frankincense and myrrh, four soft pillows, a queen's maid and court; a universal eye, an aerial car, a spiritual telephone, a spiritual airplane, celestial diamonds, celestial gold and gems of iridescense; necklaces and earrings, saffron robes, velvet robes, gold-latticed cloaks, embroidered gowns, silken gowns and slippers, wedding bands for hands and feet, pendants, amulets, lovely hair combs, silver dresses and wedding vestments, exquisite bracelets of pearls and emeralds, among other things. The Supreme is also the bestower of such names as Ma, Sita, Turiya, Brahmachari Turiya, Turiya Kriyananda,

Ramakrishna, Brahmananda, Ramnamananda, Mother Turiya Kriyananda, Mother Turiya Coltrane Kriyananda, Rami, and another name of which, and by my own election, I will eternally decline to repeat. It is a name of the highest order, and is superior to every name and gift aforementioned.[12]

At the present time, it has been my great privilege to bring certain individuals up to the high courts of the Most Holy Sovereign. Some persons are immediately permitted to enter into the Divine Presence where they receive light, love, and priceless divine instruction. Other unfortunate ones, due to their poor evolutionary spiritual state, have to remain in the outer chambers, where they receive only a small fraction of the divine light.

Moreover, I have found that some of the most fortunate individuals of all are children, especially those whose spirits have not yet been stained by impure worldly associations and undivine exposures. These fine souls go forthrightly to the Supreme Lord. They receive light and love in the fullest measure. It is like a revelation, and they are like humble revelators.

---

[12] I have recently received a fourteenth name for which I will be forevermore grateful. Although it is not the highest and dearmost name among the names given to me, it is still a wonderful name which translates as "The Transcendental Lord's highest song of bliss." The name is Turiyasangitananda.

As a result of my accompanying and directing these children to the Supreme Abode, I now thoroughly appreciate such immemorial sayings as "and a child shall lead them," "from out of the mouths of babes," and Jesus Christ's "Suffer little children to come unto me, and forbid them not: for of such is the Kingdom of Heaven . . . Whosoever shall not receive the Kingdom of God as a little child shall in no wise enter therein." Divine revelations abundantly flow from out of the pure hearts of little children, like the waters of a mighty ocean.

What is monumental and eternal to me is to feel the Lord's play and hear the Lord's laughter or talk. Why, just this morning the Lord said to me: "Hey Turiya,

At dawn, sit at the Feet of Action.
At noon, be at the Hand of Might.
At eventide, be so big that sky will
learn Sky."